Big Sailor

My First Big ABC

Ages 3-5

Vol.4 J·K·L

Milkidu!
Your study buddy

My First Big ABC Book Series
Big Sailor Edu

Copyright © 2021 Cambridge Dynasty Press

For permission requests, bulk order information, or any business related inquries, please contact the publisher at the email address below.

Cambridge Dynasty Press
30 N Gould St. STE4000
Sheridan, WY 82801
Email: Bestsailoredu@Gmail.com

Written, Designed, and Printed in the United States of America

978-1-7357844-9-6(Paperback)

47678459

Hi! Nice to meet you. My name is Milkidu!

I am your study buddy for this book!

Let's work together on this book. We will get all of these amazing educational benefits!

1. Building Skills for Pen Control
2. Recognizing Alphabet Letters
3. Building Confidence
4. Enjoying a Good Book
5. Being Patient with Practice
6. Developing Creative Thinking
7. Being Proud of Achievement
8. Having Fun

This book belongs to

_____
(name)

Let's trace following the numbers

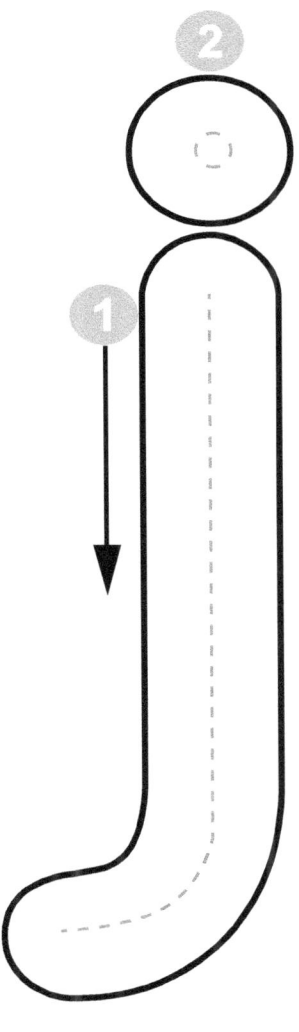

 Read out loud

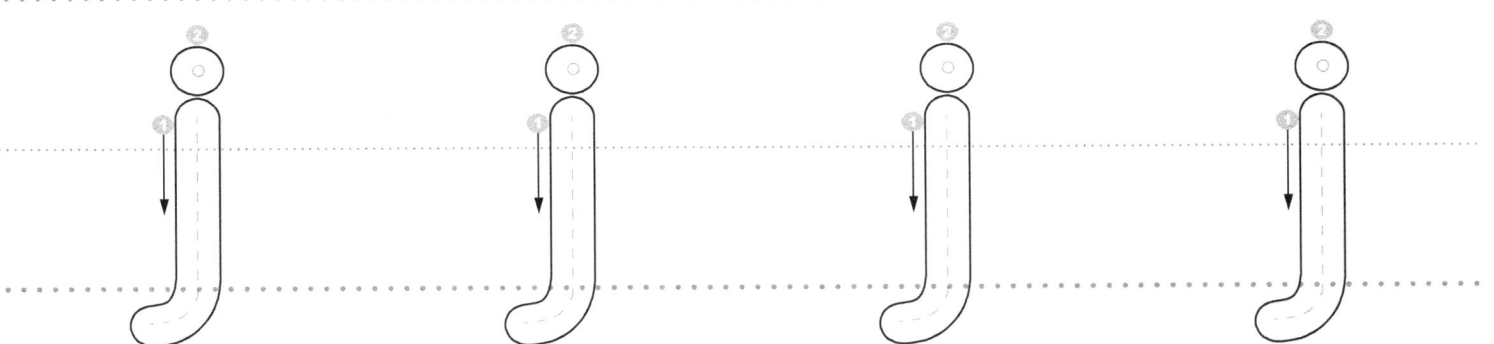

 # Juice

✏️ Let's trace following the numbers

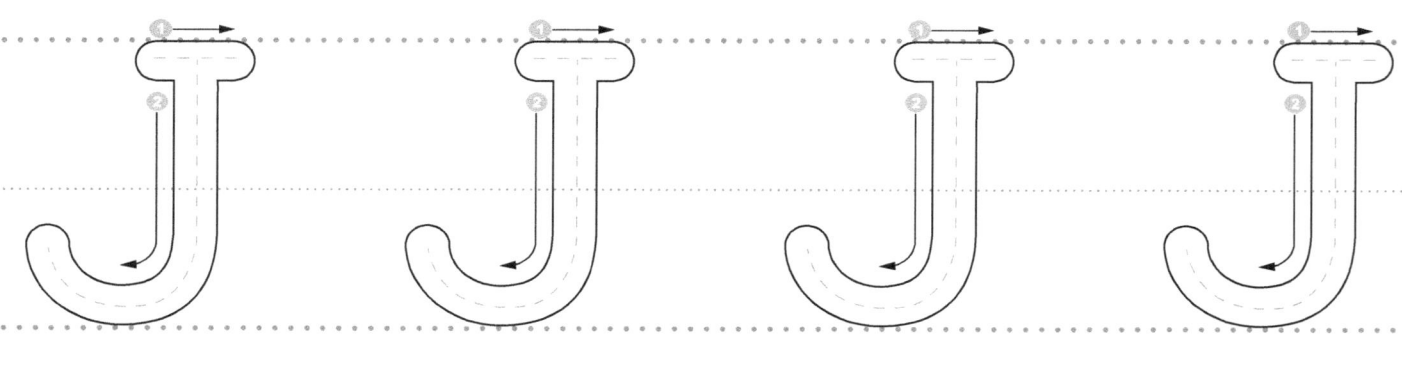

 # Jungle

jar

 Read out loud

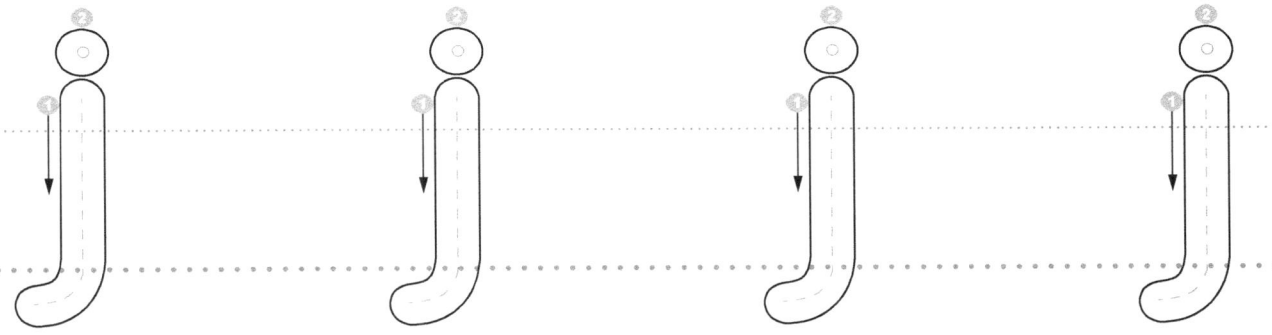

jellyfish

Find every J and color them

- A
- J
- J
- L

Trace the dotted line and read out loud

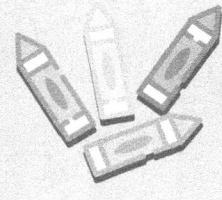 **Find every J and color the sections**

Milkidu

J
J
J
P
J
A
J
C
J
J

Find every j and circle them

j for jellyfish

Trace the dotted line and read out loud

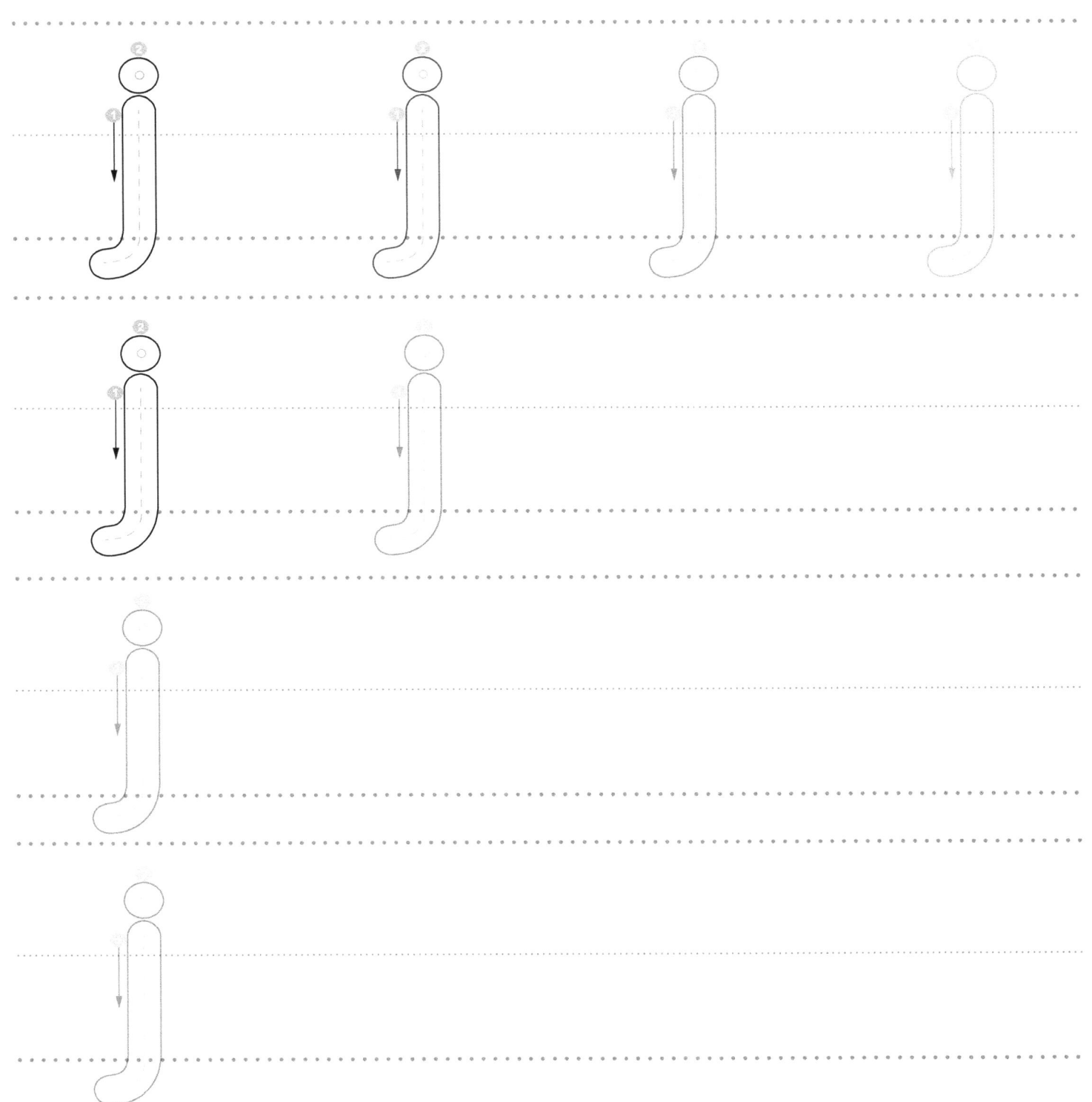

15

J for Jungle

Draw lines to match

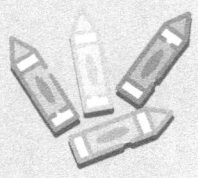 # Find every **j** and color the sections

Trace the dotted line and read out loud

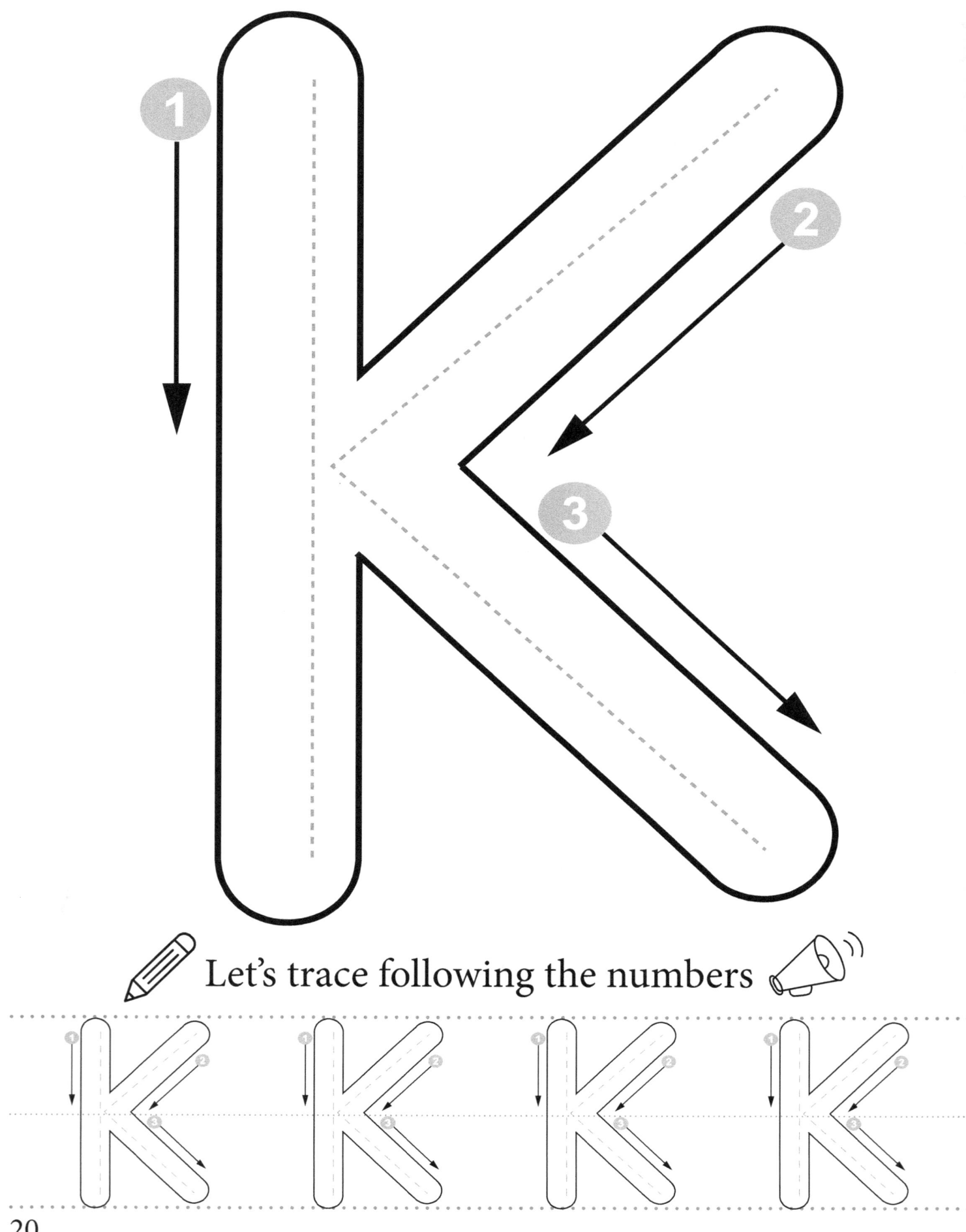

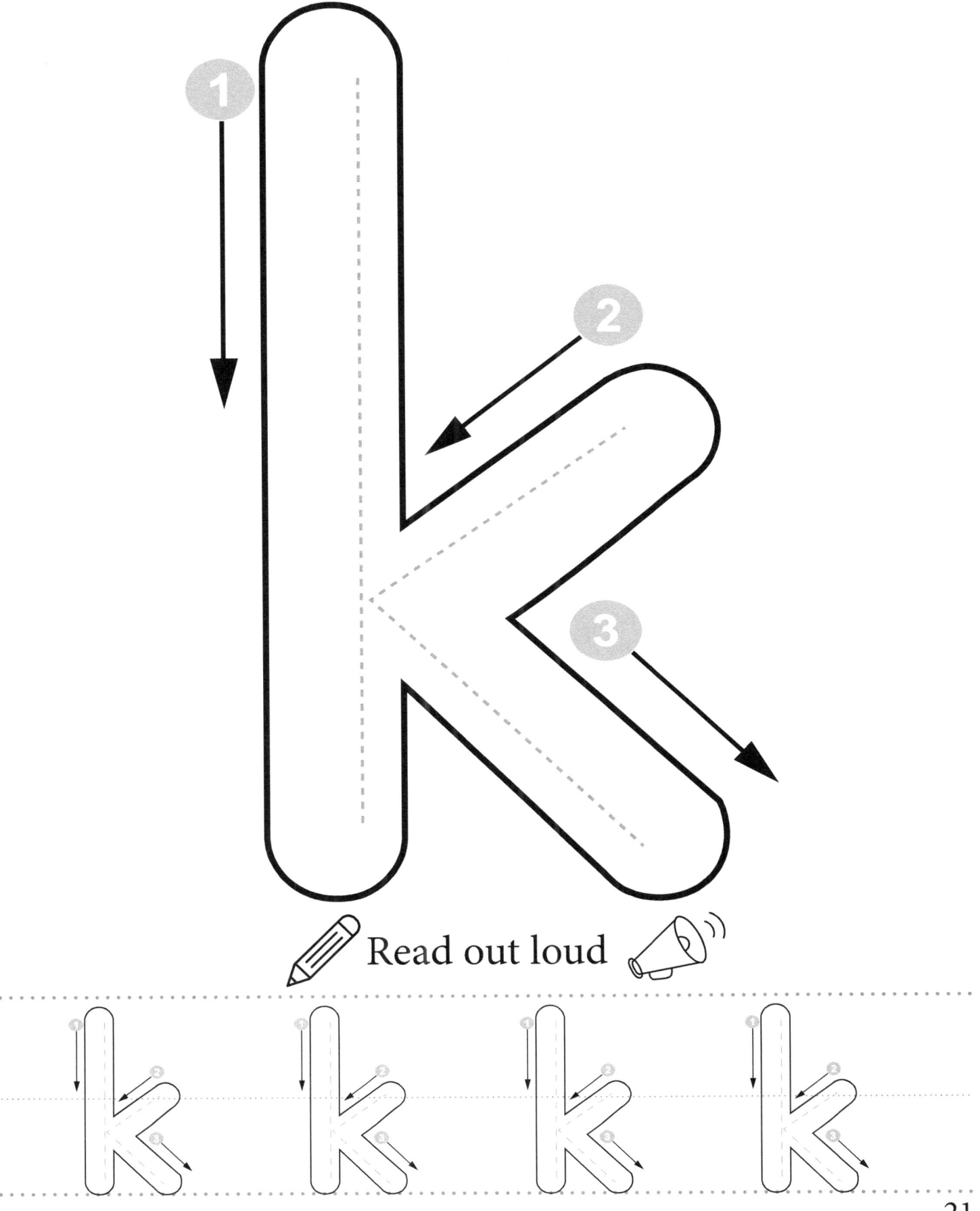

Kite

 Let's trace following the numbers

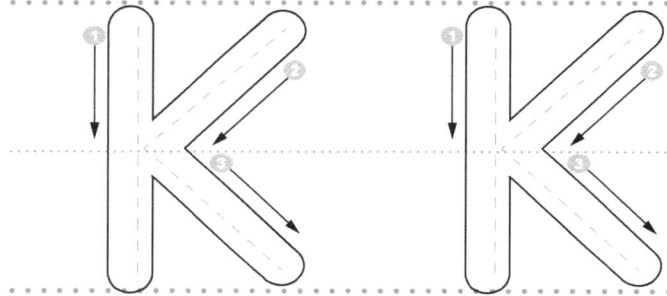

Koala

kangaroo

✏️ Read out loud 📣

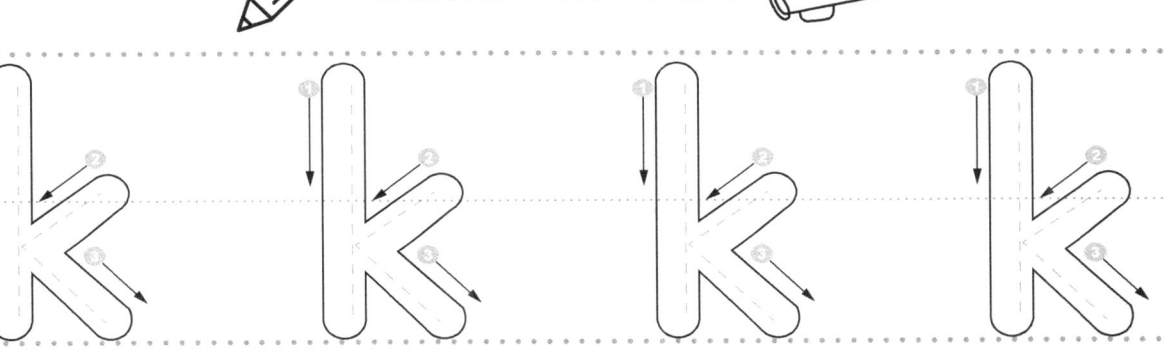

key

Find every K and color them

Trace the dotted line and read out loud

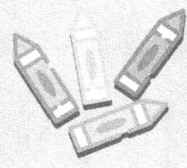 Find every K and color the sections

Milkidu

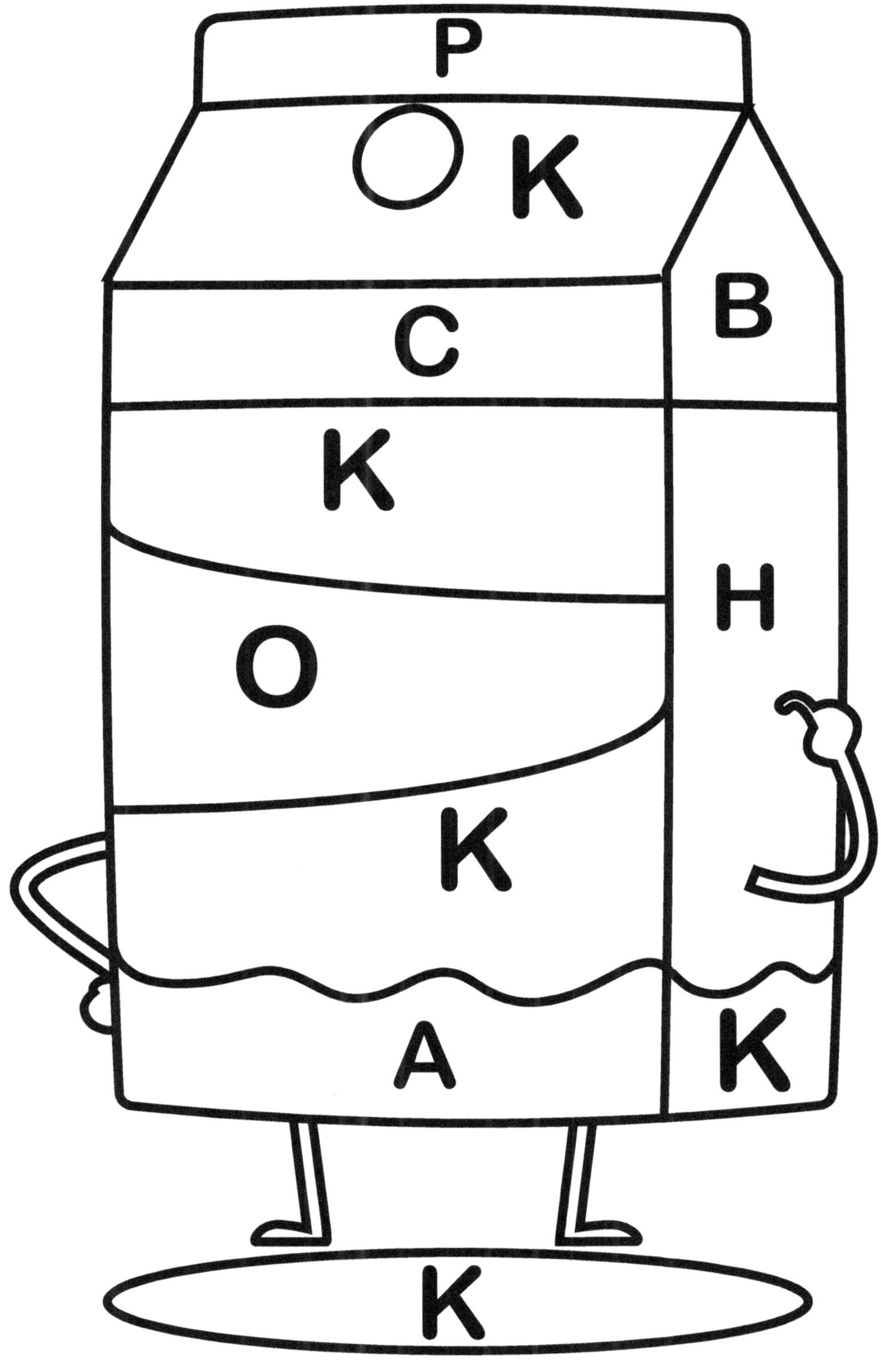

Find every k and circle them

k for koala

Trace the dotted line and read out loud

Draw lines to match

k for kangaroo

 **Find every k and color the sections**

k r k n k b k d k

Trace the dotted line and read out loud

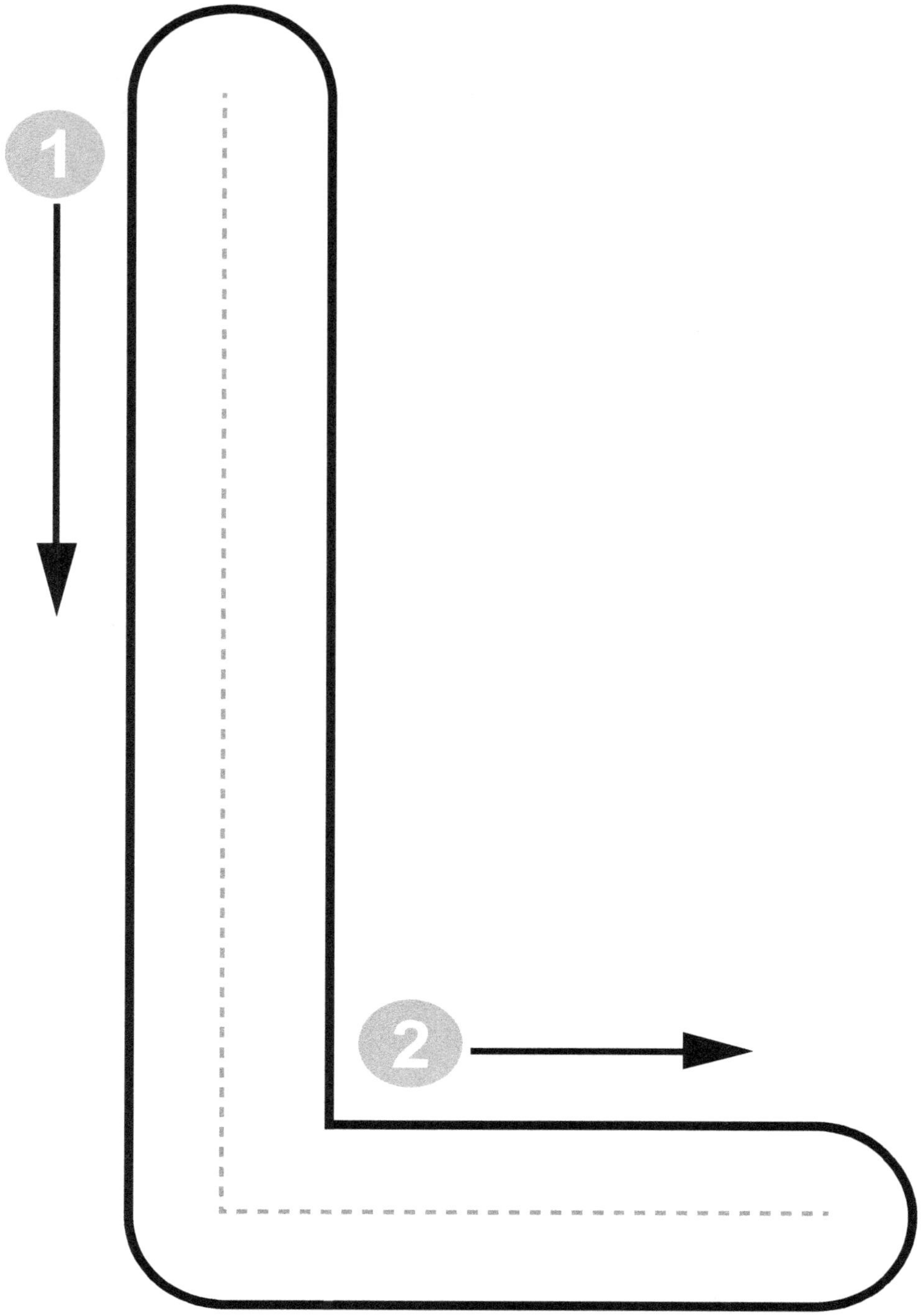

Let's trace following the numbers

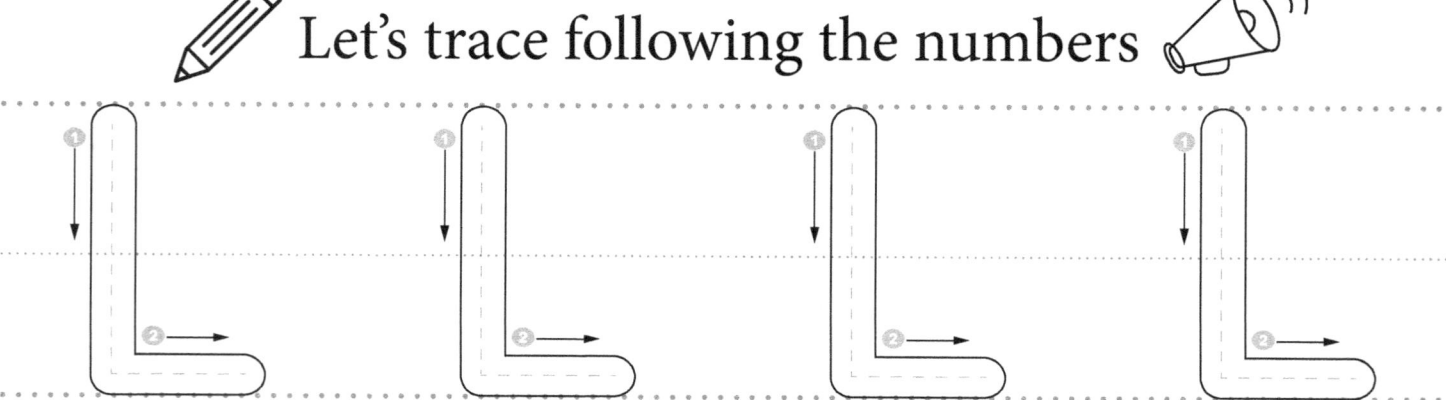

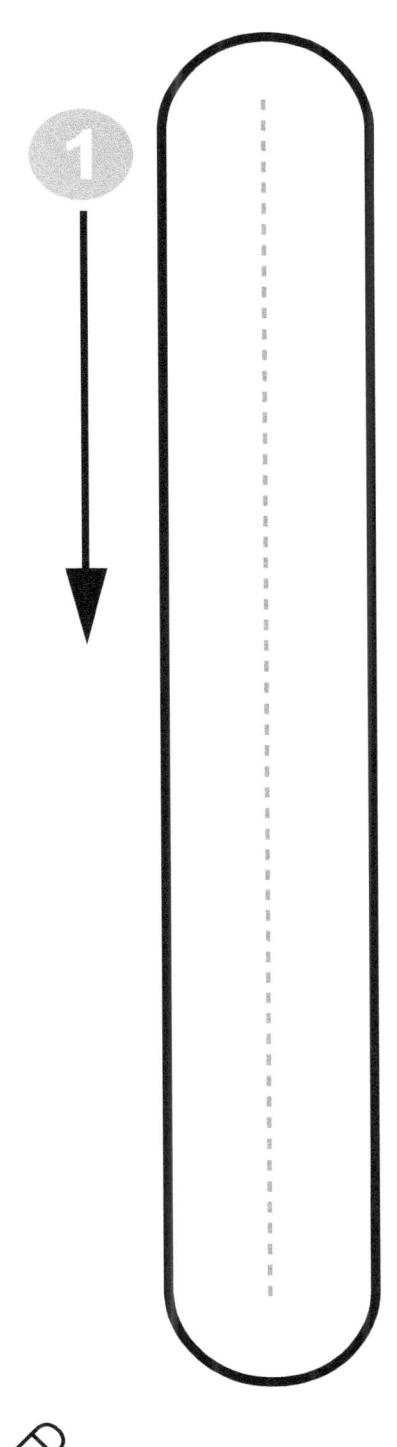

Read out loud

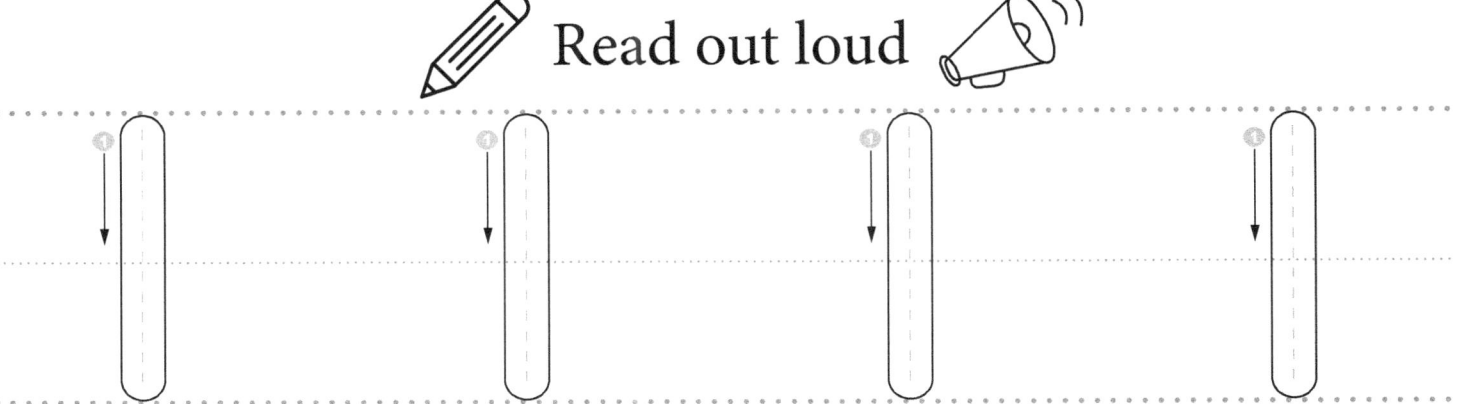

Ladybug

✏️ Let's trace following the numbers 📢

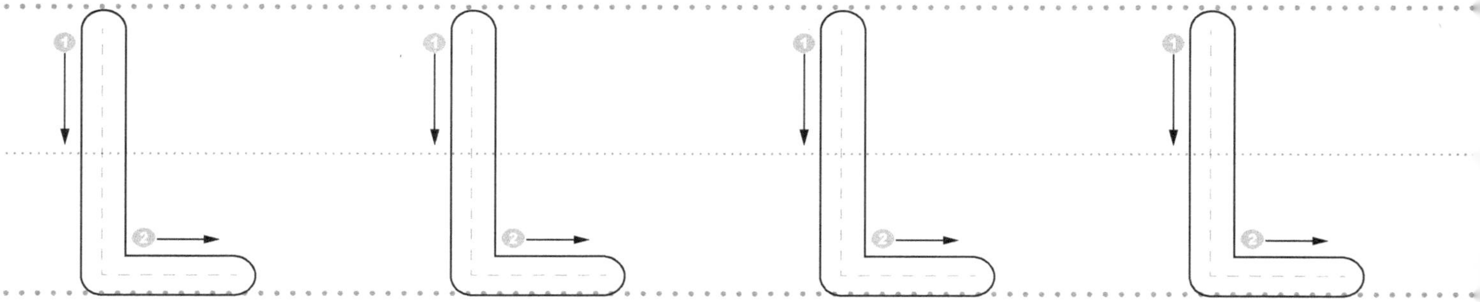

Lion

lemur

 Read out loud

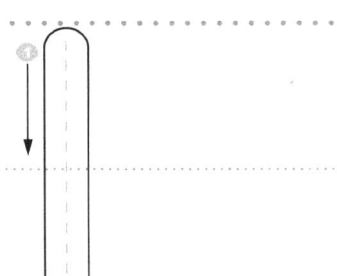

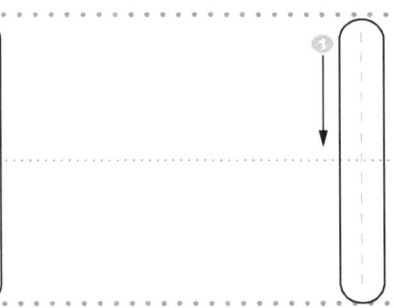

lamp

Find every L and color them

Trace the dotted line and read out loud

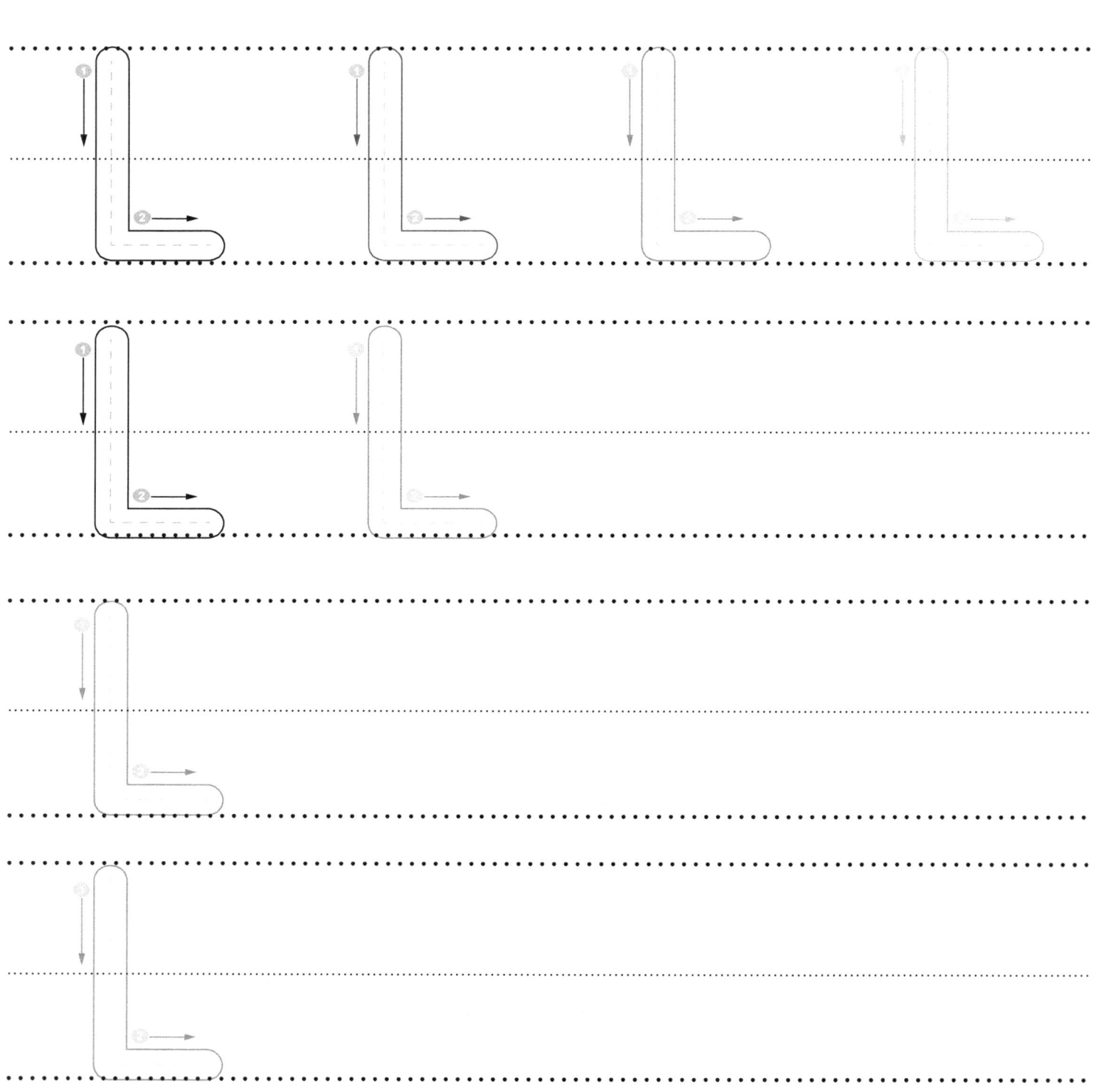

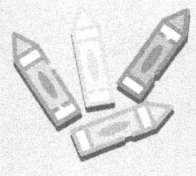 Find every L and color the sections

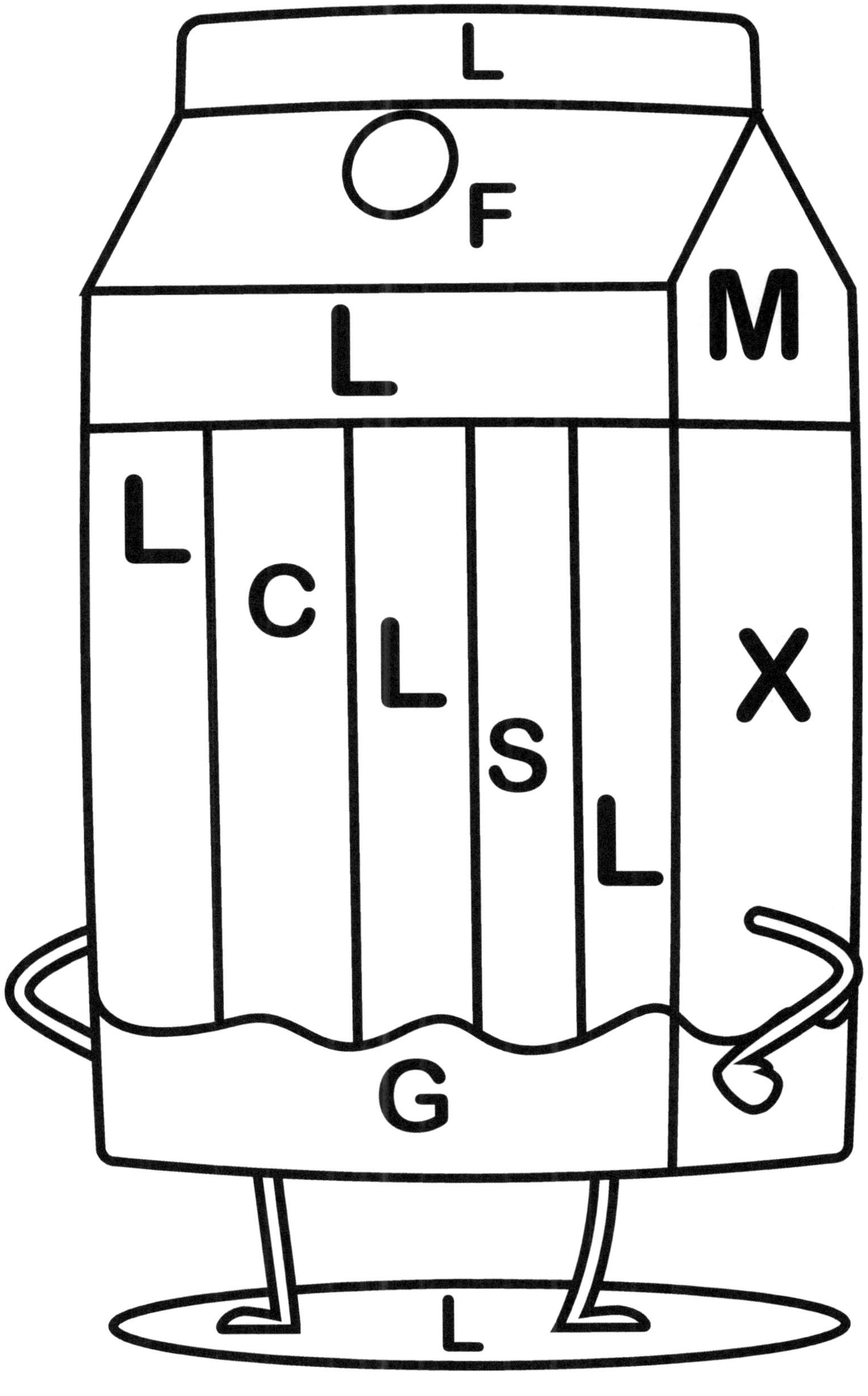

Find every l and circle them

l for lemur

Trace the dotted line and read out loud

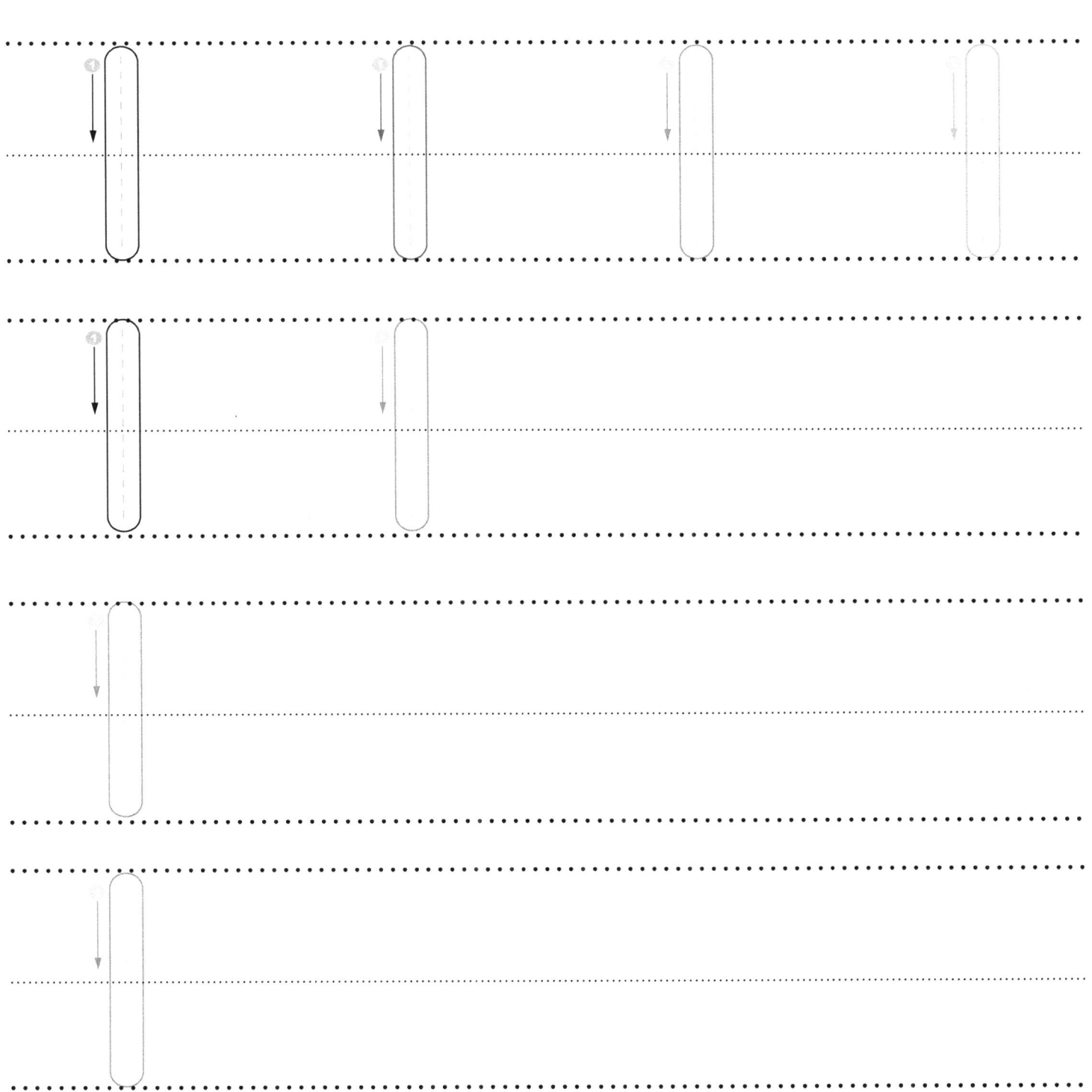

43

Draw lines to match

 **Find every l and color the sections**

Trace the dotted line and read out loud

Where is Milkidu?

Find and circle!

Let's express your

I am cool

I am hungry

I am playful

I am proud

I am okay

feelings with Milkidu!

I am tired

I am excited

I am loved

I am confident

I am happy

Let's express your

I am sad

I am calm

I am rushing

I am frustrated

I am angry

feelings with Milkidu!

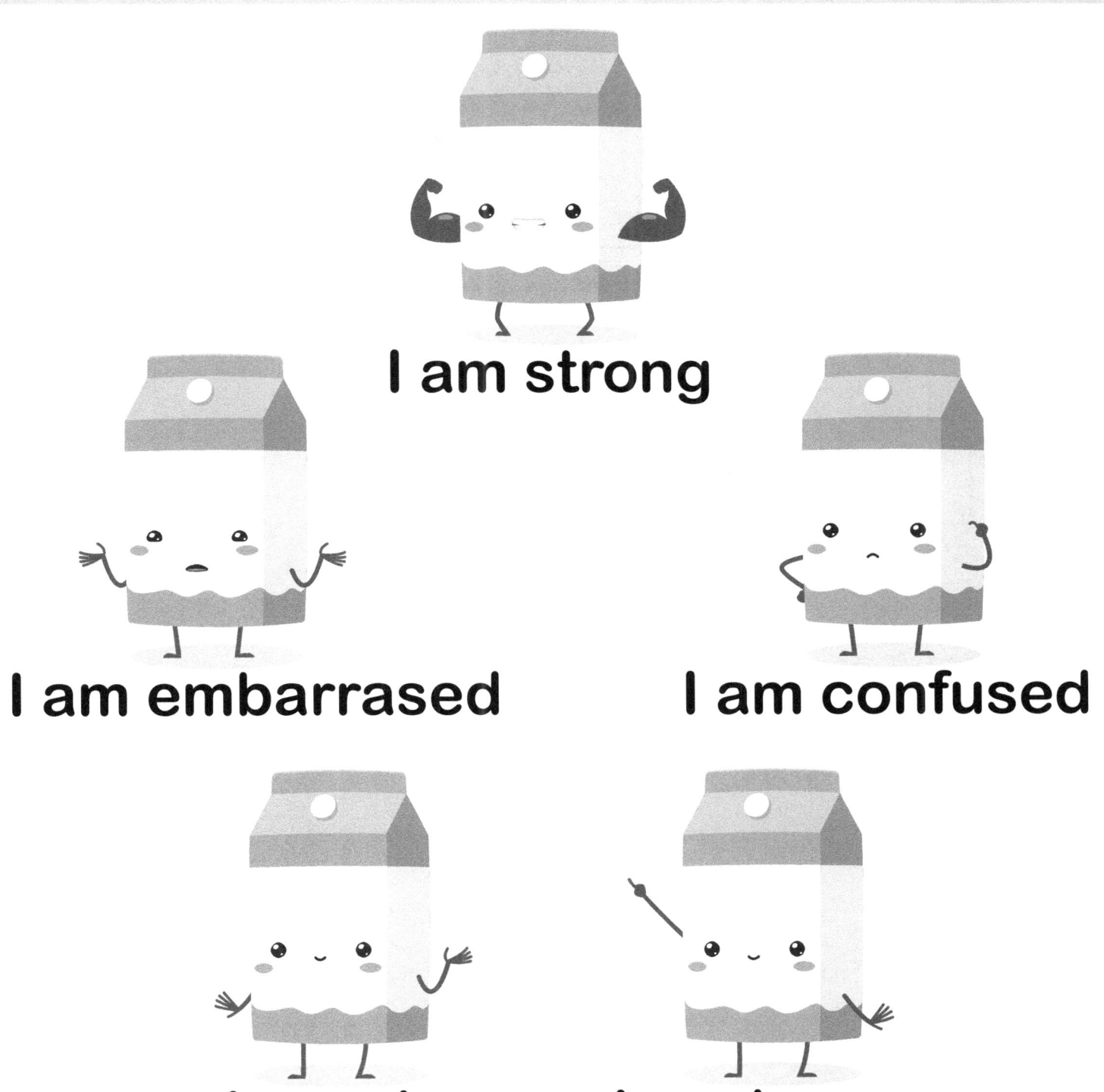

Write JKL and read out loud

JKL JKL

JKL

JKL

JKL

Write jkl and read out loud

Award

You are amazing!

This award is for

_____ _____
(first name)   (last name)

Great job finishing the book!

Date: _____

Visit Our Website

BigSailorEdu.com

and Get Free & Fun

Educational Material

ABC Workbook Series by Big Sailor Edu

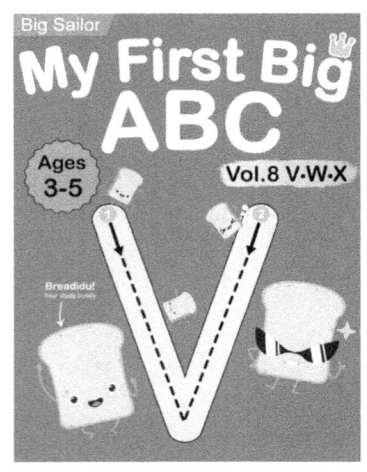

Cambridge Dynasty Press

www.ingramcontent.com/pod-product-compliance
Lightning Source LLC
Chambersburg PA
CBHW081421080526
44589CB00016B/2628